PLATFORM SHOES

Ray Ellsworth

A Big Step in Fashion

Schiffer Publishing Ltd

4880 Lower Valley Road, Atglen, PA 19310

DEDICATION

This book is dedicated to
William A. Stepanek
without whom it would not have been possible.

Copyright © 1998 by Ray Ellsworth
Library of Congress Catalog Card Number: 97-80254

Book design by Blair R. Loughrey

ISBN: 0-7643-0459-3
Printed in Hong Kong
1 2 3 4

Published by Schiffer Publishing Ltd.
4880 Lower Valley Road
Atglen, PA 19310
Phone: (610) 593-1777; Fax: (610) 593-2002
E-mail: Schifferbk@aol.com
Please write for a free catalog.
This book may be purchased from the publisher.
Please include $3.95 for shipping.

Please try your bookstore first.

We are interested in hearing from authors
with book ideas on related subjects.

ACKNOWLEDGMENTS

I would like to thank Peter and Nancy Schiffer for all their help in making a long-time dream come true and all the other people at Schiffer Publishing who helped put it together. Also, a great many friends have supported me over the years, and I would like to thank particularly Larry and Randy Rubin, Bev Williams, Candy Cooper, Judi Triest, See Goldi Last (The Queen of Dania), Louise and Jim Revells (The Straw), Helene M. Weiss, Pat Seddon, Barbara Beale, Lois Perito, Natalle Ross, Elton John, Dorothy Loud, and Michael Bentley and Anna MacPhail who literally drove me to do this book. Special thanks go to Cora Wujceak for giving me a new lease on life and to my mother, Constance Ellsworth, and my sister, Virginia Breer, for their constant love and support which gave me the strength to follow my dream.

CONTENTS

Opposite:
Silver sequin tie-ups made for Di Orsini, 4 1/2," 1970s, USA. $200

Silver and black with ankle straps and hearts, Lerness Shoe. This is the highest platform in this collection and was the second pair collected. Beginner's luck! It is the most coveted pair of all; everyone wants to have them.

6

Pink rubber platform sandals with
floral printed fabric thongs. $45

INTRODUCTION

platform n. **4 a:** a usu. thick layer (as of cork) between the inner sole and outer sole of a shoe **b:** a shoe having such a sole

— *Webster's Ninth New Collegiate Dictionary.*

People tell funny stories from their experiences with platform shoes. They remember where and when they bought their first pair, and what happened next. It's hard to catch a cab in New York wearing them. Since they aren't made for long distance runs, an awful lot of us recall when they broke, often causing a good laugh and a snicker.

Some people call platform shoes "Carmen Miranda" shoes, but in viewing her movies, you can't really see anything that looks like a platform. Maybe it's the whole look of the forties they're thinking about, and Carmen was about as outrageous as any of them knew.

Your parents always warned that you'd break your neck in them. That didn't happen, but they were duly rebellious and wearing platforms was just tons of fun.

Platform shoes have been around as dancers' costumes for many decades, but have been popular among consumers only periodically. They were widely accepted in the 1940s, and frequently encountered again in the 1960s. At other times they fell

Red leather
with black
glitter and
silver flowers.
This was the
first platform
shoe the
author found
and it started
his collection.
$250

Red and white sling backs with round white heels, Bubble Shoe. This style reminds one of the little Nash Ramblers of the 1950s. $150

far out of favor so that even great designs were ignored by most shoppers. In about 1984, a pair of snazzy men's platform boots was noticed in a high-price booth at an antiques show. Intimidated by the other prices around them, the collector almost walked by without inquiring how much they were. But he persisted, and was told, "Oh, you can have *them* for $4."

Kids today like to borrow the old ones for costume parties. Young girls love them and want the new ones in all their different forms.

The estimated values reflect the retail market as it is known to the author for similar shoes at the time of publication. No responsibility is taken for their future accuracy.

Now we all cherish platforms because they are so memorable. This group has been enthusiastically assembled one pair at a time over a twenty-five year period, and the collection isn't done yet. "Step right up" and enjoy them!

![N logo]

NOVELTIES

A pillow, just for fun. This was the most asked about shoe in the collection. If there were 20,000 people through the shop, 19,000 asked about this one.

The smallest pair of platforms, about the size of your thumbnail. Originally they may have been a pair of earrings for pierced ears. These were a gift.

A little thong style sandal with layered rubber platform, fashioned into a key chain. There is also a two-foot long sandal of this same style that must have been a display pair, or meant for a giant.

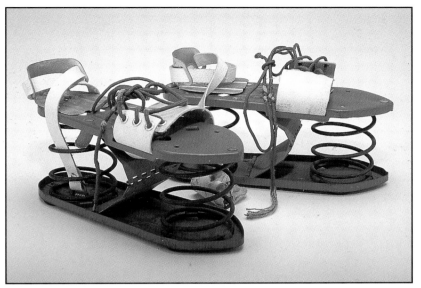

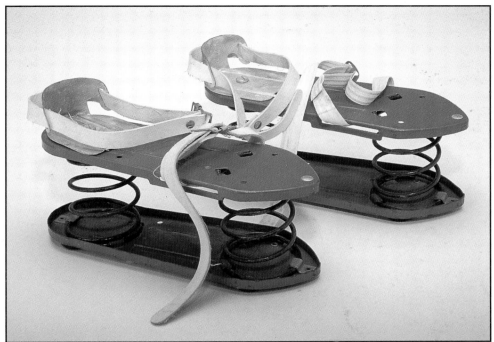

Above and right:
Two modified versions of the spring shoe with a more balanced design, and they actually went into production.

Album covers with platform shoes featured on them are few, but fun. Presumably the records provide music for stepping high.

A fabric jacket with shoes design including a platform pair.

13

T
TIE-UPS

Leather
checkerboard
tie-ups. $95

Brown and black
leather tie-ups.
$125

14

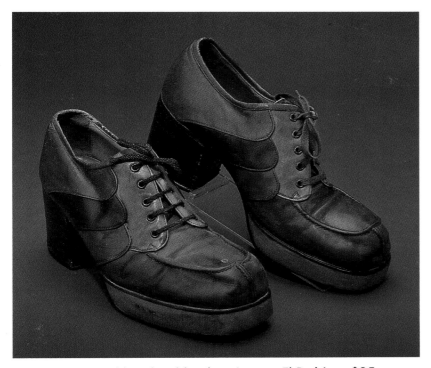

Brown, gold and red leather tie-ups, El Padrino. $95

Black and burgundy leather tie-ups. $100

Verde black and brown leather tie-ups, 1970s. $95

Bonitas curved heel, brown and black leather tie-ups, Brazil. $100

15

Black tie-ups with
silver trim, Lerness
for West Flagler, in
really nice shape.
$200

Very
sturdy
brown
oxfords.

Brown tie-ups
sold by
Montgomery
Ward. $125

Platform wedge tie-ups by Rudolf Valentino, blue with green beads and white pearls. $100

Blue leather tie-ups with orange trim, El Padrino. $125

Fantasia green cloth with tan leather tie-ups. $125

Tartan plaid and black leather tie-ups. $75

17

Black leather
tie-ups with a
5" heel. $85

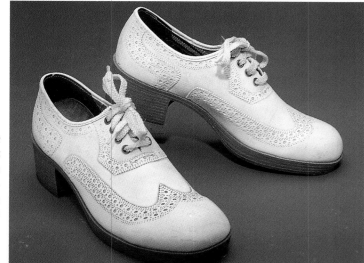

White
plastic
wing-tip
style tie-
ups, Green
Shoes. $75

GullenKamp,
Brazil brown
leather tie-ups.
$65

18

Brown leather tie-ups, Mr. Man, Spain. $150

Brown leather tie-ups with nice detailing. $65

Brown leather tie-ups, Brute's, Poland. $85

19

Black leather tie-ups,. $125

Red leather tie-up with an up-turned toe that gives a sculptural look to the design. $65

Black leather tie-up uppers with brown bottoms, Made in Spain. $85

Blue glitter tie-ups with white bottoms. $85

Black leather tie-ups with white stitching and an up-turned toe, 1970s. $150

Three-toned brown and white leather tie-ups with layered bottom,. $85

Red suede tie-ups
with black laces and
an open toe,. $50

Opposite:
Red corduroy tie-ups
with a 4" heel. $125

Silver sequin tie-ups for Di Orsini,
4 1/2" heels, 1970s, USA. $200

Light blue and black leather
tie-ups, Flagg Bros. $95

23

Silver leather with burgundy patterned fabric
sides, tie-up laces, and open toe. $85

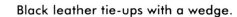

Black leather tie-ups with a wedge.

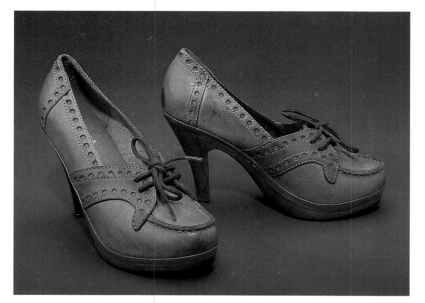

Town and Country tan leather
tie up with leather laces. $75

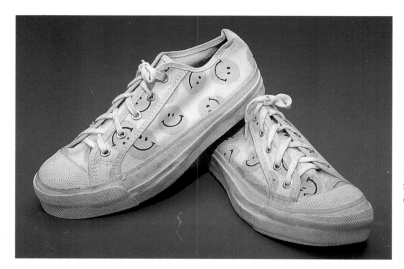

Happy Face
sneakers,
Converse.
$60

Green suede tie-ups with a geometric design, Edouard Jerrold, Greece. $75

Black, green, brown and red leather patchwork tie-ups with 6" heels. $150

Black and white leather tie-ups. $150

Black leather openwork lace-ups with open toes. $75

BOOTS

White leather
Go/Go boots.
$85

Multi-colored
patchwork leather
boots with side
zipper, 1970s. $100

Black leather and suede boots with side zippers. $100

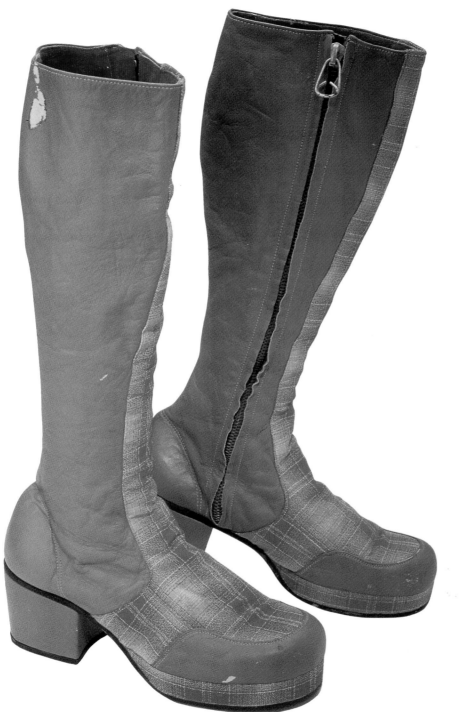

Grey leather boots with red and white plaid fabric inserts and side zipper, Bob Prima Shoes. $250

Brown patchwork leather boots, tie-up closure and unusual round heels, 1970s. $150

27

Snake skin boots, 21" high, with a side zipper,. These belonged to an exotic dancer. $250

28

Above:
Red suede boots with gold
leather platform and heel, Made
in England, 20" high. $150

Right:
Brown leather boots with a
side zipper and angled top,
22" high,. $150

29

Red leather clogs,
Tomaia Pelle Pola
Pensato. $75

CLOGS, SCUFFS, AND MULES

Clogs have open backs but closed toes, and the bottom is inflexible and usually made from wood. The type derives from Dutch wooden shoes. Similar to a clog, but with a flat, non-wooden sole, is a *scuff*. Then a *mule* is high heeled and backless, with or without a wooden sole.

Black patent leather clog, Famolare Italy. The owner calls them the Frankenstein shoes because they make you walk with a lurch and would be great for Halloween. Everyone wants to try them on, but they are a small size. $200

Brown interwoven leather clogs with tassels, Buskems. $50

Quali Craft clogs of woven leather with buckle trim and pierced wooden soles. $50

White vinyl top clog. $60

Brown leather and fringe clogs with pierced wooden soles, by Quali Craft. $60

31

Red glitter clogs,
Rosane, Brazil. $65

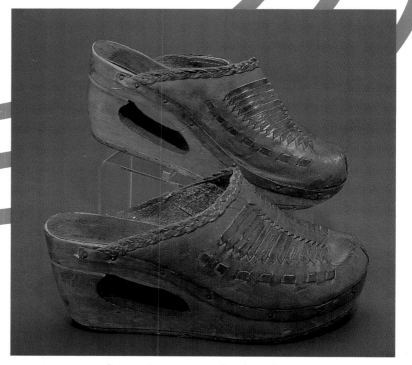

Brown interwoven leather clogs
with pierced wooden soles. $50

Brown interwoven
leather clogs with
tassels, Buskems. $50

Brown leather mules with silver studs and wooden soles with an unusual round heel, by Martinelli, Italy. $95

Red patent leather clogs with silver studs. $65

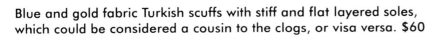

Blue and gold fabric Turkish scuffs with stiff and flat layered soles, which could be considered a cousin to the clogs, or visa versa. $60

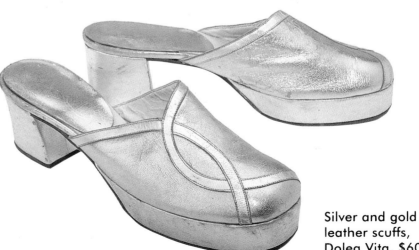

Silver and gold leather scuffs, Dolea Vita. $60

33

Turquoise leather all around, including the 5 1/2" heel, Let's Go, Firenze. $85

Decorated red suede mules, Allabouts, Greece. $85

Brown leather high heel mules with wooden soles and 5" heels. $75

34

Red leather mules. $85

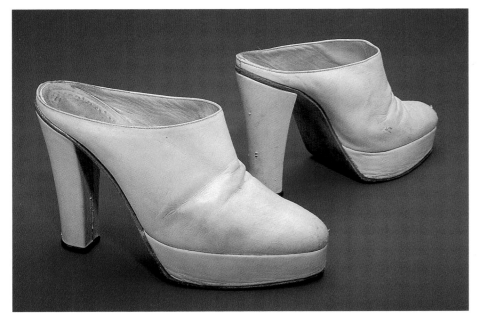

White leather high heel mules, 1970s. $60

Sheepskin high heel mules with wooden soles. $65

35

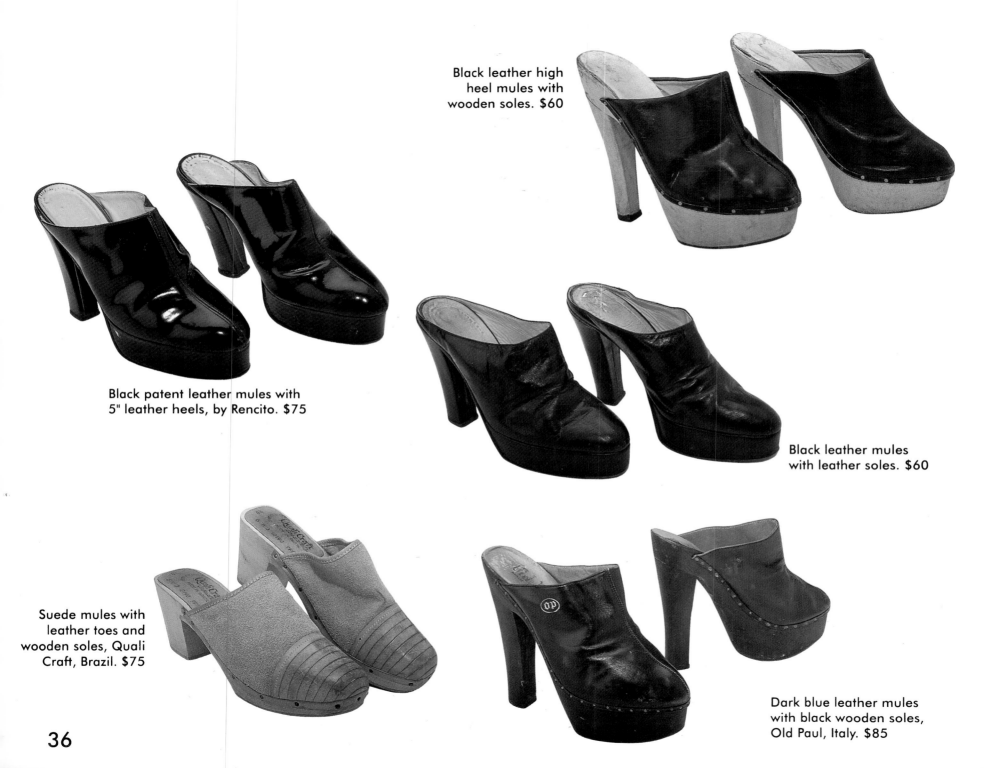

Black leather high heel mules with wooden soles. $60

Black patent leather mules with 5" leather heels, by Rencito. $75

Black leather mules with leather soles. $60

Suede mules with leather toes and wooden soles, Quali Craft, Brazil. $75

Dark blue leather mules with black wooden soles, Old Paul, Italy. $85

36

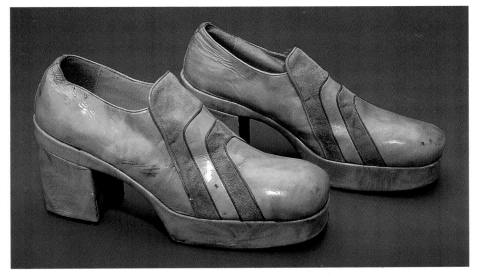

Light brown leather slip-ons with grey suede stripes and a wooden sole. $100

SLIP-ONS AND SANDALS

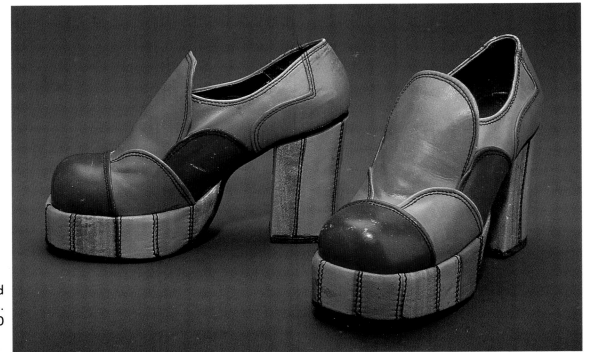

Multi-colored leather slip-ons. $100

38

Blue polka dot fabric slip-ons with red patent leather trim and rubber soles, Eppy and Eppy, Spain. $150

Opposite:
Cork soled slip-ons of burgundy, green, and gold leather tops with side buckle trim and a trapezoid heel, French Room. $175

Multi-colored leather slip-ons, El Dita's, Spain. $100

Blue, pink, and black slip-ons. $100

Red leather slip-ons with mirrored pieces set in a design, some pieces missing. Used in the film "Revenge of the Nerds," 1983. $125

Brown leather slip-ons with sequins and red stones decoration, some missing. These appeared in a dance scene of the movie "Revenge of the Nerds," 1983. $125

Right:
Tan leather slip-ons with leopard fur trim and belted closure. $95

Below:
Brown wedge slip-ons with cork soles. $60

Two-tone blue leather slip-ons, 1970s. $95

Dark green leather wedge slip-ons with cork soles, Italia. $60

Yellow patent leather slip-ons with mock laces. $85

White leather slip-ons that remind the owner of the dance sequence in Pee Wee Herman's movie where, to the music "Tequila," he tried to escape conflict with a group of bikers. These special shoes inspired the popularity of white loafers. $85

White leather slip-ons, Italy. $85

42

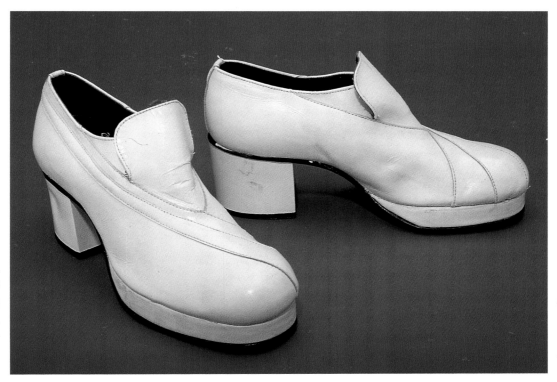

White leather
slip-ons of
sculptured
design,
Milano. $125

Black leather slip-ons with black, beige and green
striped woven soles, Volpe Imperial, Italy. $150

White leather slip-ons, 1970. $95

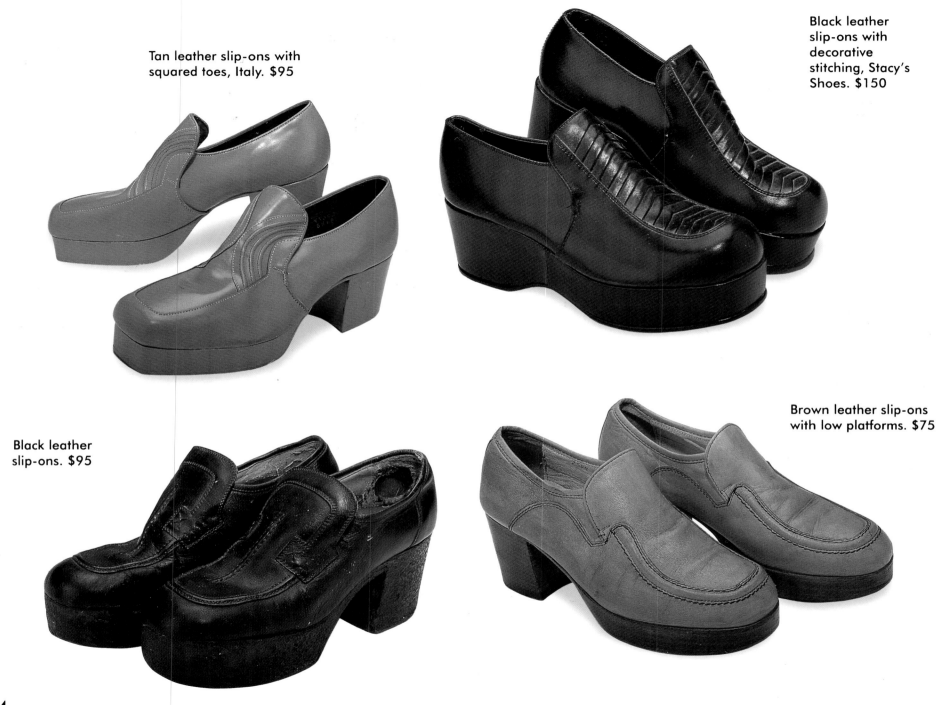

Tan leather slip-ons with squared toes, Italy. $95

Black leather slip-ons with decorative stitching, Stacy's Shoes. $150

Black leather slip-ons. $95

Brown leather slip-ons with low platforms. $75

Brown leather slip-ons with 5"
heels and 2" high toes. $150

Black leather low platform slip-ons, Truitt. $95

Blue leather
slip-ons, Volpe,
Argentina.

45

Brown reptile skin slip-ons with fringe and tassels. $100

Black reptile skin slip-ons with smooth toes, fringe and tassels. $100

Blue leather slip-ons with round heels. $75

Black leather pumps with flowers hand-painted, 5 1/2" heels, Creca Shoes, Made in Greece.

Turkish bizarre platform slip-ons of finely tooled leather and contrasting stitching. These are quite old. $150

Snake skin, slip-on, platform pumps with solid heel and enclosed toes, Kings Highway, The Shoe Box. $100

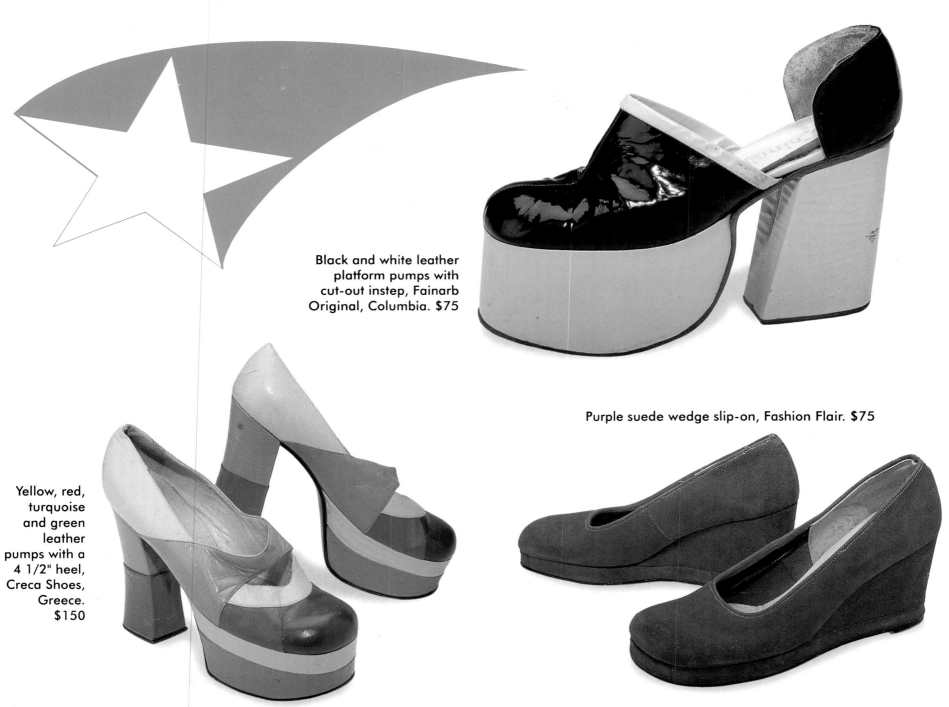

Black and white leather platform pumps with cut-out instep, Fainarb Original, Columbia. $75

Purple suede wedge slip-on, Fashion Flair. $75

Yellow, red, turquoise and green leather pumps with a 4 1/2" heel, Creca Shoes, Greece. $150

48

Dark blue leather pumps. $65

Red and yellow leather pumps by Erich Prince Ilia, Brazil. $150

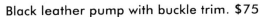

Black leather pump with buckle trim. $75

Black leather pumps with snake skin trim and 4" heels, Patent Leather Bootery Jamar. $150

Red leather pumps with black glitter and silver flowers. This was the first pair the author found and it started his collection. $250

Black leather, open toe pumps with silver trim. $150

Black patent leather, open toe platform pump, Projections. $85

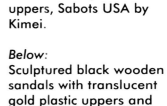

Left:
Sculptured wooden sandals with translucent tortoise shell plastic uppers, Sabots USA by Kimei.

Below:
Sculptured black wooden sandals with translucent gold plastic uppers and silver-head upholstery tacks. $75

Sandals:
slip-ons with open heels and open toes

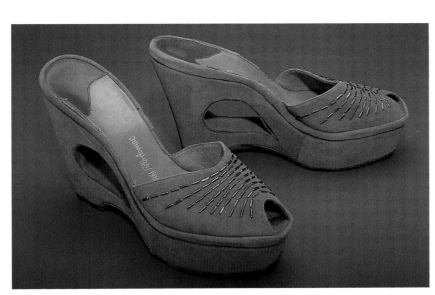

Pink suede sandals with beaded toes and pierced heels, Saks Fifth Ave. $65

Pink wooden sandals with hand painted floral decoration. $65

Wooden sandals with white macrame uppers and carved heels. $50

Wooden sandals with pagoda carved heels and beaded toes. $75

Brown leather
and cork
wedge platform
sandals. $75

Rust suede and tan leather wedge sandals
with crochet trim, Neiman Marcus. $85

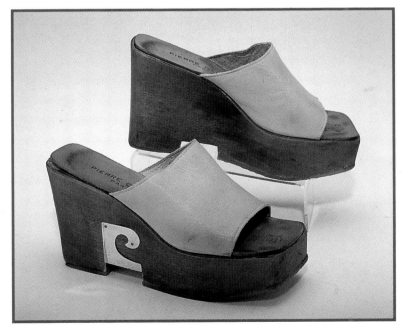

Tan leather wedge sandals,
1970s, Pierre Cardin, Paris. $75

53

Brown leather and
black wooden 6"
high heel mules,
Old Paul, Italy. $65

Cream colored leather and black wooden
high heel mules by Old Paul. $60

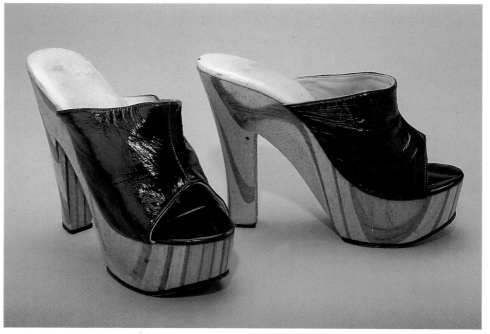

Dark brown leather and wooden
high heel mules. $75

54

Black and white
woven leather
mules with 3 1/2"
high scallop-
decorated heel
and sole,
Bovrovki, Made in
Greece. $60

Light brown leather mules with 4" heels,
Bibiana's By Famolare, Italy. $75

One-piece, brown molded
plastic mules with cork insoles,
The Haloit For El Grees by
Christian Vermong. $60

55

Red, blue and gold leather mules with white piping and wooden heels and soles. $65

Brown interwoven leather sandals with pierced wooden soles, India. $75

Peach and green leather mules with wooden heels and soles, Lit Brothers. $65

Red and white leather high heel sandals. $65.

Brown and white floral print fabric sandals with woven wedge platforms.

High heel sandals with hand painted leather straps and wooden platform, Argentina. $75

57

Gold and leather straps sandals with gold over cork platforms, Charles Jourdan, Paris. $50

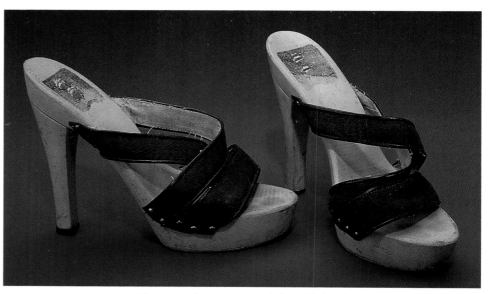

Blue suede strap sandals with high wooden heels and platform. $60

Green and gold leather strap sandals with gold, wing-carved wooden heels, Keng. $65

Black wooden platform sandals with white leather straps and buckle closures, 1970s. $50

Black and white checkerboard leather sling backs, 1997, with 5" heels. $40

SLING BACKS

slip-ons with heel straps

Orange leather sling backs with colored circles on the toes, Classics, Italy. $75

Red and white sling backs with round white heels, Bubble Shoe. This style reminds one of the little Nash Ramblers of the 1950s. $150

Brown leather sling backs, Ward. $75

Black suede sling backs with snake skin toes, Goody Two Shoes. $85

Black patent leather sling backs with ribbed cork soles, Italy. $75

Gold leather sling backs with strap toes, Lima-Peru. $85

Silver leather sling backs, 1970s, Angel Hair. $75

Red, blue and black
plaid fabric sling backs
with woven straw
wedge platforms. $60

Blue suede sling back sandals by Di Orsini. $100

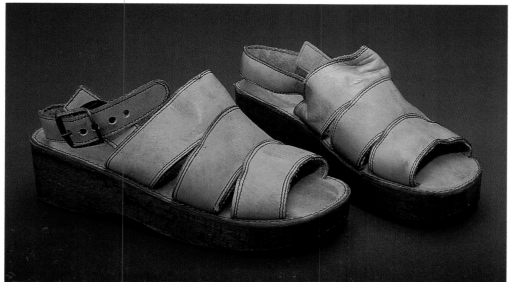

Tan leather sling
back sandals
(open toes),
Thom Mcan. $65

Above:
Red satin sling back
sandals with silver and
gold embroidered
flowers and 4 1/2"
heels. $125

Right:
Black satin sling back
sandals with gold and
silver embroidered
flowers, 1970s,
Wilbar's. $100

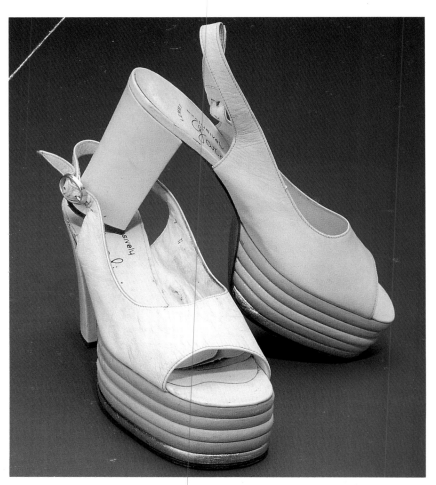

White leather sling back sandals with multi-colored platform sole, Garolini, Italy. $75

Black and silver leather with 6" heels and 3" high toes, Lerner Shoes. $175

Grey and black suede sling back sandals. $85

Above:
Red, yellow, blue and white leather sling back sandals on high wooden platforms, Rapallo. $75

Left:
Black and brown leather sling back sandals with high, wooden, 5" heels, by Raphael. $85

Right:
Green and cream leather, sling back platform sandals with great detailing of white dots. $75

Below:
Red bandanna print, sling back platform sandals. $75

WEBSTER LEWIS

ON THE TOWN

AND THE POST-POP SPACE-ROCK BE-BOP GOSPEL TABERNACLE ORCHESTRA AND CHORUS

Brown leather sling back, wedge sandals. $60

Graceful, pink leather, sling back sandals, 1970s. $75

Brown leather sling back sandals with square heels, Wild Pair, Brazil, 1970s. $65

Brown leather sling back sandals with interwoven crossing straps. $75

Black leather sling backs with braided straps and wedge platforms. $65

White leather sling backs with crossing straps, Made in Brazil. $50

Brown leather sling backs with interwoven straps. $85

White straps and sling backs on raffia woven platforms, Flamenco of Spain. $85

Brown suede platforms with white buckled straps. $75

Molded platform, sling back sandals with red checked fabric bows. These are the ones to wear to that diner with the red checked tablecloths. $85

Vinyl snake skin and white leather sling back sandals, Biarritz, Spain. $150

Braided hemp straps and wooden platforms in a sling back sandal design, Brazil. $85

Interwoven braided hemp, sling back sandals, Classics by Morse. $50

Black and glitter "spider web" sling back sandals, Lady McGuire. $75

Gold leather, sling back, wedge platform sandals with woven straps. $75

Blue suede straps criss-crossing on a low platform, sling back sandals, Duco 5th Avenue. $65

Silver leather, sling back, wedge platform sandals with woven straps. $75

T

T-STRAPS

straps forming a T at the instep

Black leather, t-straps, Gaymode, J.C. Penney. $85

Burgundy leather t-straps, Rossi. $50

Black and white check fabric t-straps. $85

72

Black leather and wooden platform, t-strap sandals with high heels. $85

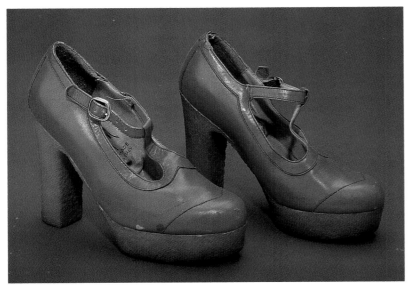

Red leather t-straps by Joseph. $75

White leather t-strap platform with open toes. $65

White leather t-strap sandals with wooden platforms, 1970s, Naughty But Nice. $100

Black leather t-strap sandals with pierced wooden platforms. $95

Brown leather and interwoven raffia t-strap sandals, Young and Fare, Italy. $50

Multi-colored leather platforms with ankle straps and 5 1/2" heels, Emma of London. $175

Black gathered leather low platforms with ankle straps by Spatafora. $75

Pastel colored snake skin platforms with ankle straps, Jerry de Havilland for Dany's. $85

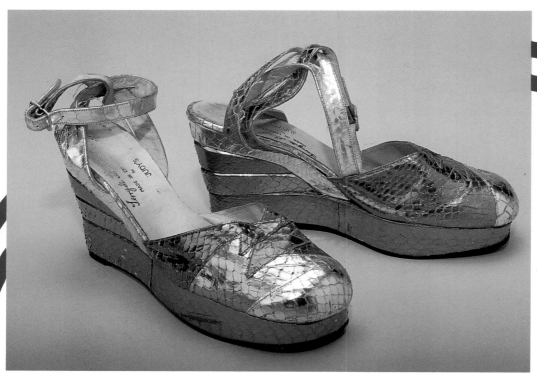

Multi-colored, metallic, snake skin patterned leather, wedge platforms with ankle straps, Jerry de Havilland. $95

Black patent and red leather wedge platforms with ankle straps, Made in Greece. $125

Beige leather with ankle straps and open toes, wooden block heels, and yellow platforms, 1970s, Projections. $125

Beige leather and dark brown platforms with 4" heels, Socialites. $50

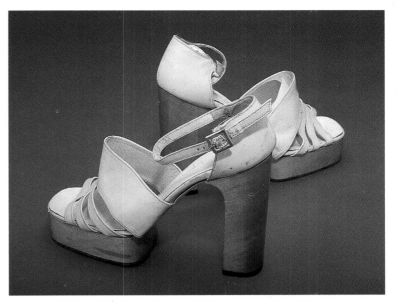

White leather shoes with instep and ankle straps and wooden heels and platforms. $75

Right:
Black leather ankle strap sandals with green, gold and red toe accents and 6 1/2" heels, Goody Two Shoes, N.Y.C. $175

Below left:
Brown leather ankle strap sandals with striped wooden heels and platforms, Young Californian Shoes Inc., Designed in Calif. Made in Republic of China. $75

Snake skin and black leather ankle strap sandals on striped wooden 4" heels and platforms. $85

Red satin ankle strap sandals with wooden platforms, by Raphael. $75

Wooden platform sandals of red leather with ankle straps, Miss Constance, Brazil. $85

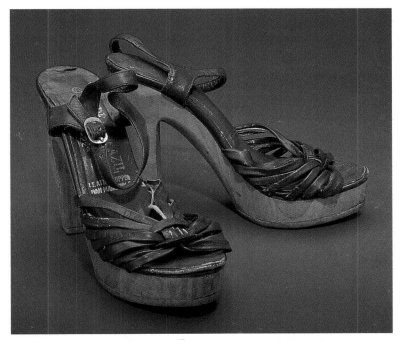

Burgundy leather ankle strap sandals with wooden platforms, Made in Italy. $85

Wooden platform sandals with black suede and ankle straps, Joseph for Cherokee.

Brown leather ankle strap sandals with set-in design, attached with upholstery tacks to the wooden platforms. $75

Wooden platform sandals with 5" heels, red leather ankle straps, and clear vinyl toe straps decorated with artificial fruit and berries and attached with small upholstery tacks. $75

82

Brown leather ankle strap sandals attached to beige plastic platforms with upholstery tacks, by Quali craft. $85

Wooden platform sandals with green leather ankle straps and toe straps with white stamped decoration attache with upholstery tacks, 1960s. $75

Green and yellow leather strap sandals attached with gold colored upholstery tacks to the wooden platforms, Garolini, Italy. $85

83

Zebra striped wooden platform sandals with black leather toe and ankle straps, DiOpsim, Spain. $95

Black wooden platform sandals with buckled, brown leather toe and ankle straps. $100

White leather ankle strap sandals with wooden platforms, 1960s. $75

84

Brown woven leather ankle strap
sandals, Made in Taiwan. $75

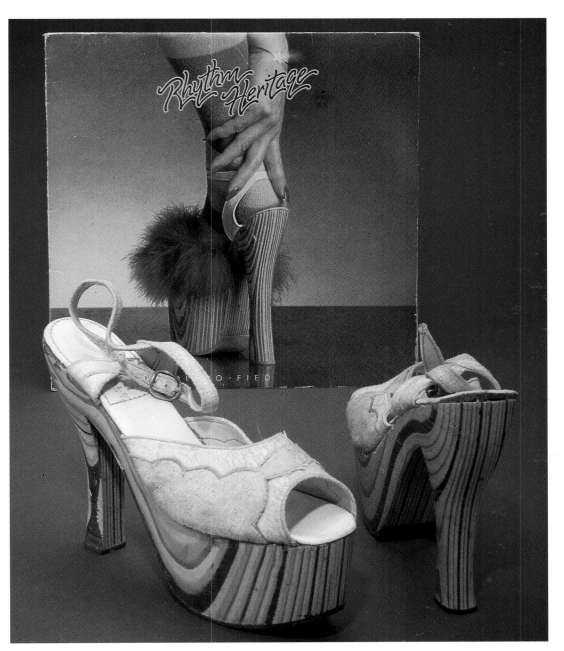

Zebra wood platform sandals with tan suede and
leather toe and ankle straps, Botticelli, Spain. $125

85

Left:
Dark blue suede ankle strap sandals with black laces and scroll carved wooden platforms, Librettos. $125

Below right:
Brown leather ankle strap sandals on pierced wooden platforms, India. $65

Wooden platform sandals with silver leather ankle straps and gold glitter toe straps, Stuff by Frank Sbicca. $75

Brown suede ankle strap
sandals on wooden platforms
with donut cut-out heels,
Puppy Shoes, Spain. $85

Above:
V-back, wooden platform sandals with
brown suede toe and ankle straps, Puppy
Shoes. $150

Lerft:
Black ankle strap sandals on wooden
platforms with pierced heels, The Wild
Pair, Made in Brazil. $75

V-back, wooden platform sandals with yellow leather ankle straps and clear vinyl toe straps attached with upholstery tacks and decorated with artificial flowers. This pair looks like modern sculpture. $135

Dark blue leather, ankle strap sandals with cork platforms, Saks 5th Ave. $75

Red floral fabric ankle strap sandals with cork platforms, Chandelle. $95

Green and yellow leather, ankle strap sandals with multi-colored woven toe strap attached with upholstery tacks, El Dita's, Made in Spain. $125

Brown leather ankle strap sandals on a platform base of contrasting cork layers.

Red patent leather ankle strap sandals with cork platforms and 4 1/2" heels, late 1960s. $85

89

Silver leather ankle strap sandals with crossover toe straps. $75

Snake skin ankle strap sandals with four colors and white piping on high heeled cork platforms. $75

Red leather ankle strap sandals on cork platforms with 4 1/2" heels and 3" toes. $125

Right:
Red velvet ankle strap sandals with silver glitter flowers on the platforms, Miles. $125

Below:
Burlap and raffia ankle strap sandal with raffia laces and deep platform. $75

Red bandanna fabric ankle strap sandals on woven raffia covered platforms. $75

Grey leather ankle strap sandal on woven raffia platform, Vino. $75

Red and yellow woven raffia ankle strap sandals on wedge platform. $75

Brown leather ankle strap sandal on raffia woven platform, Carber. $75

Right:
Pink floral printed fabric ankle strap sandals with 5" heels and matching fabric bows on the toes. $85

Below:
Green satin ankle strap sandals with green satin bows on clear Vinyl toe straps and black platforms. $95

Black, green and purple metallic snake skin ankle strap sandals with Vinyl toe straps, Jerry de Havilland, London, England. $85

Silver leather ankle strap sandals with high heel and clear Vinyl toe strap, Flamencos. $60

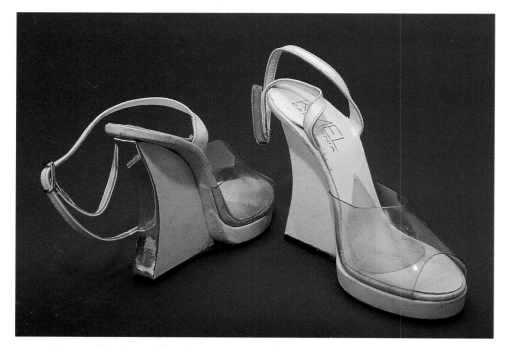

Unusually shaped heels appear on these white leather and chrome ankle strap sandals with Vinyl toe straps, Kimel, California. $75

94

Orange leather ankle strap sandals with Vinyl toe panels and orange platforms. $85

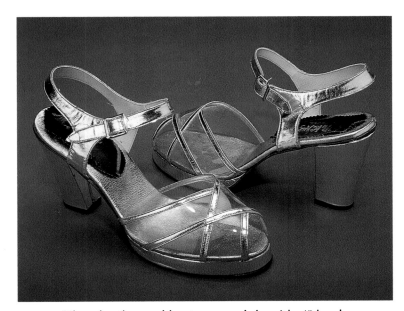

Silver leather ankle strap sandals with 4" heels and clear Vinyl toes, Capricho's, USA $60

Black platforms with 6" heels, silver leather ankle straps and trim on the clear Vinyl toes. $125

Silver leather ankle strap sandals with 5" heels and straps tied at the toes, Thom McAn.

Black suede ankle and toe strap sandals. $60

Red suede platform sandals with red leather ankle straps and clear Vinyl toes with red satin ribbon flower heads, Florett. $95

Blue leather ankle strap sandals with red stripe on the toes. $125

Green suede ankle strap sandals, Mandels of Calif. $85

Silver sequins platform with 5" heels, silver leather ankle straps and bow on the clear Vinyl toes, Imperial Quality Fashion. $95

Gold leather
ankle and toe
strap sandals
with open toes.
$75

Above:
Black leather ankle strap sandals
with bows on the toes, Italy. $125

Right:
Light blue leather ankle strap
sandals with a flat black bow on
each toe and 5 1/2" heels. $85

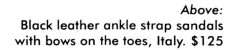

Black suede and leather ankle strap sandals with 6 1/2" heels and 3" high toes. $150

White leather ankle strap platform sandals with white polka dot bows, Designed by Erich Prince Ilia, Brazil. $100

Red suede ankle strap sandals with 5" heels, Vinbaker, Italy. $85

Beige suede platform with tan leather ankle strap sandal. $65

Black suede ankle strap sandals with silver studs decoration, H. Anton Martinez Elda, Espana. $85

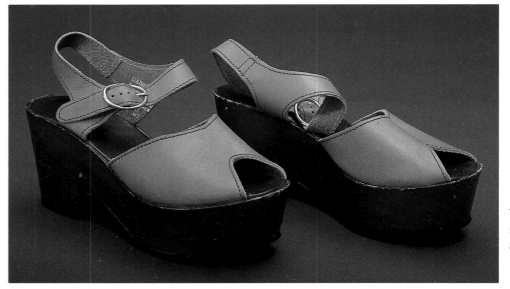

Tan leather ankle strap sandals, Made by Jiff. $65

Beige leather, open toed, high heel, ankle strap sandals, Lornes, Handmade. $125

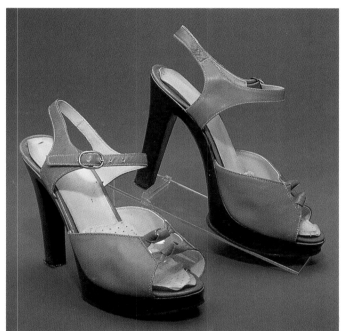

Brown open toe, ankle strap sandals on high, black heels and platforms. $75

White leather, high heeled ankle strap sandals by Quali Craft. $65

Multi-colored snake skin, ankle strap sandals, Galliano, Phillipines. $85

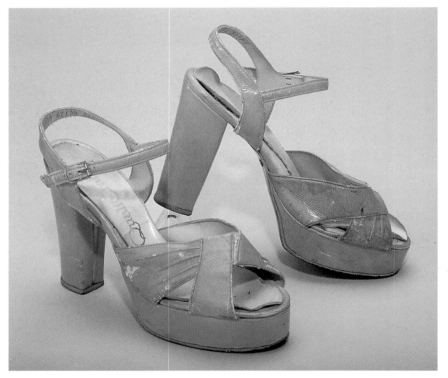

Beige leather ankle strap sandals with high heel and platform, Quali Craft. $60

Red leather ankle strap sandals with 5 1/2" heel, Pama the Cred, Italy. $60

Red velvet ankle strap sandals with red and blue floral design, by Silvio, Italy. $125

Blue denim ankle strap sandals with a red strawberry appliqued on each toe. $50

Blue leather platform ankle strap sandals with multi-colored woven fabric toe straps, Goody Two Shoes, N.Y., 1970s. $15

Right:
Brown leather ankle strap sandals with dark brown floral design on the platforms and 5" heels, New Look, Greece. $95

Below:
Black leather ankle strap sandals with hand painted flowers on the 6" heels and toe platforms. $125

Dark blue satin ankle strap sandals with hand painted pagoda scenes on the heels and platforms. $85

Black velvet ankle strap sandals with floral embroidered toe straps and carved and painted wedge platforms with cut-out heels, Phillipines, 1970s. $85

Below:
Floral print fabric ankle strap sandals with 5 1/2" heels and wedge platforms. $125

Black and pink leather ankle strap sandals with an embroidered scroll design on the platforms and heels. $85

107

Green velvet ankle strap sandals with glitter flowers on the wedge platforms. $85

Floral printed fabric, ankle strap sandals with wedge platforms, First Editions. $95

Black sequined ankle strap sandals with 6" heels. $85

White leather open toe, ankle strap sandals with a peacock in a tree painted design on the platforms, 1970s. $95

Black ankle strap sandals with black and white sculptural decorations on the toe straps, 5" heels on the wedge platforms and plastic, movable eye spots. These are the original "I'm keeping an eye on you" shoes. $75

Black crush patent leather ankle strap sandals with bows at the toe straps and 5" high, floral fabric covered, wedge platforms, Urbana. $100

Gold fabric ankle strap sandals with green on the straps and 5 1/2" high wedge heels, California Clogs. $100

Gold leather and glitter ankle strap platform sandals, Fantasies of Fashion, USA. $85

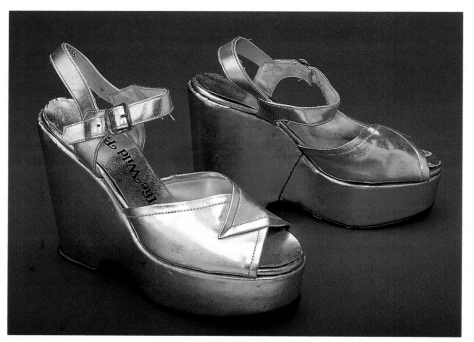

Silver leather ankle strap sandals with 5 1/2" high platforms, Wild Pair. $85

110

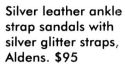

Silver leather ankle strap sandals with silver glitter straps, Aldens. $95

Above:
Sliver glitter ankle strap sandals with high platforms. $95

Left:
Silver leather ankle strap sandals with silver glitter platforms, Balenciaga. $95

Silver leather ankle strap sandals with red suede high platform and black widow spider motif on the heels. $85